I0483935

HOME BUYING:
MASTER THE PROCESS

LEARN TIPS AND SECRETS ONLY REALTORS AND LENDERS KNOW!

DAVID VAN WALDICK

Website: SimpleStepsHome.com
Email: dave@wrfco.com
Phone: 888-930-4223

LEGAL NOTES

Copyright © 2015 by David Van Waldick

WRFCO MEDIA
701 PALOMAR AIRPORT RD., #300
CARLSBAD, CA 92011
PUBLISHING@WRFCO.COM

INTRODUCTION

After 20 years, and successfully closing 1,500 mortgage and real estate transactions totaling over $1 BILLION, I felt knowledgeable enough to write about the process of home buying, and how to approach it.

By far, the single biggest mistake real estate professionals make when working with homebuyers is the failure to educate them in advance about the process and needs of home buying. By reading this book and listening to our step-by-step home buying process education series, would-be home buyers can familiarize themselves with the needs and process, and increase their control and success rate when it comes to buying a home.

TABLE OF CONTENTS

Legal Notes 2

Introduction 3

Table of Contents 4

Chapter 1 5

Why Be A Homeowner? 5

Chapter 2 Loans: It's All About the Financing! 7

Chapter 4...42

Chapter 5...46

Chapter 6...47

Chapter 7...48

Chapter 8...49

Chapter 9...51

Chapter 10 53

About The Author 54

Simple Guide Books By David Van Waldick........55

Can I Ask A Favor? 56

CHAPTER 1
WHY BE A HOMEOWNER?

Before we embark on the home ownership journey, as with any worthwhile endeavor, we have to first ask ourselves to be clear about the goals and benefits.

The benefits are many. While there are certainly pitfalls and ongoing efforts and costs to maintain a nice home for yourself and your family, the benefits far outweigh the problems.

Financial Stability

Studies show homeownership to be the cornerstone of financial stability. When purchasing the right home for your budget and needs, there is no better way to ensure that your family will be financially secure in the long run. Not only will your home provide physical shelter, but the connections built within the family and neighbors will continue to benefit you for the rest of your life.

Of course, we anticipate the home will appreciate over time, and over the course of ownership, you will pay down your loan until the day you can burn your mortgage deed. Whoohoo!! Plus, any physical improvements or additions typically add value.

One of the financial benefits not available to renters, but afforded homeowners, is the mortgage interest deduction. You can actually reduce your annual income tax bill by a significant amount through an IRS ruling that allows you to reduce your taxable income dollar for dollar, and hence the amount of taxes you pay at year's end. This also allows W-2 wage earners to take additional tax withholdings from their monthly paychecks, which has the effect of providing you a higher monthly paycheck than if you did not own a home. At year's end, your tax specialist will work through all the adjustments to balance your annual tax bill and savings.

Security

Owning your own home truly makes you the king or queen of your castle. You can install whatever you feel is necessary to make it physically secure including fencing, locks, video security, and any sort of armed response security that makes you comfortable.

Freedom - Decorating, Remodeling, Room Additions

We have all wanted to decorate or remodel our apartment or rental home, only to be stopped because the landlord will not allow it, or we don't want to invest in someone else's home. Once you own your own home, you can do whatever strikes your fancy, from top to bottom design and decorating. We can go on and on about the benefits of ownership, but you already have the desire to own so let's get to it.

CHAPTER 2
LOANS: IT'S ALL ABOUT THE FINANCING!

As the saying goes, it's all about the financing, and that is absolutely right. Once we have properly planned for our home financing and determined the maximum loan amount (and thus the purchase price we can afford), we are then in a great position to go find the house of our dreams. We can confidently write offers knowing we will be approved for financing, and close on time.

Thus, the best way to buy a home is to have a sound, verified financial strategy. In other words, to be "pre-approved," as we say. That is to have a mortgage lending underwriter review and verify our financial information, and ability to qualify for the loan and close on time as per our offer contract.

Credit

Any experienced loan officer will begin by asking about and pulling your credit report. That is our starting point. More loans are denied due to bad credit or poorly resolved credit issues than any other reason. Most people have a general feel for their credit history, but often do know specifically what their credit report tells the lender.

Use of Credit

Credit scoring models and underwriters not only consider credit history and scores, but look closely at the level of credit usage. Heavy users of credit, especially when younger, are a bad indicator to an underwriter even when scores are adequate. It tells them that the borrower is likely to get into trouble down the road when a mortgage payment is placed on top of a tendency to heavily rely on credit for purchases or living expenses. To put a number on that, if you have three or more credit cards, lines, payment plans, etc., it is critical to pay off, consolidate, and close the extra ones, even if the balances are low or zero. Underwrites know how easy it is to get additional credit.

Last, when it comes to credit usage, consider your credit activity "frozen" for three to six months prior to the time you want to get a loan pre-approved. Any new accounts are a red flag to the underwriter. Just go without until you close and move in before taking out credit of any kind including new credit cards, auto loans, or personal loans of any sort.

Credit History

Credit history, or the line-by-line creditor report of balance, payments, and any late pay, is a direct reflection on a borrower's ability to handle financial obligations responsibly. So, some credit is necessary to reflect a stable credit management history. As already discussed, too much credit is not good. We will discuss credit "derogs," or bad credit, and what, if anything, you can do a little further along in this book.

Credit Scores

What are scores? Mortgage scores, i.e.,"credit scores," are comprised of collection and reporting activity of the three main national credit bureaus Experian, Equifax, and Transunion. These three bureaus collect and report an individual's credit history, and have complex statistical models used to develop an individual's credit score at any given time. Credit scoring for mortgage loan approval is different than that for auto loans, consumer credit, or credit cards.

How are Credit Scores Used?

Of the three scores received, the mortgage underwriting systems uniformly use the middle score (i.e., 680,693, 705; thus the middle score of 693 is used), of the primary borrower to determine score eligibility. Some exceptions apply, but this is the general rule.

Raising Your Scores

Low credit scores from late payments, clerical errors, past B/K's, etc., can be raised by contacting the individual bureau with a good dispute or data error plea. Because this is time consuming and requires strong knowledge of credit and reporting methods, it is best left to a credit clean-up company. Costs for credit cleanup can go from zero to thousands of dollars, depending on the complexity of the cleanup. These activities are best performed at least 6-12 months out from applying for a loan to be most effective.

Names on Report

Credit reports often contain multiple names, which confuse the underwriter and typically reduce scores. The most mixed names come from spouses, ex-spouses, and family members with similar names, like father and son with same first names.

Serious Credit Derogatory Events

Bankruptcies, prior short sales/foreclosures, credit charge-offs, IRS liens, and child support liens are examples of serious credit events that can stop a mortgage request immediately if not handled properly. Some of these events have actual timing benchmarks that must be met to proceed. Example, a bankruptcy generally requires two to three years from the discharge date to allow a mortgage.

Child liens can be complex, and can take two to three months to resolve. Each of these has its own need to be resolved. Again, the rule of thumb is to attack it early—at least 6-12 months prior to wanting to buy a home.

Income

Types

With the various types of income a homebuyer may receive, each has its own effect on the qualifying and underwriting process. Generally, buyers will have one or several of these income payment types.

Hourly / Salary

The most common type of income is hourly or salary, in which case the underwriter will use the most recent paystubs to determine current income. He or she will also look at year-end W-2's, and the most recent year's tax return to determine consistency of income. Large changes or gaps in income or employment will be viewed negatively and can effect current income qualifying.

Commissions & Bonuses

Commissioned income and bonuses by nature are less consistent in both frequency and level. Therefore, the underwriter must average these income types over time. The typical time line is to use the most recent past two years of tax returns, plus any recent year-end income statements that may have been received. This two-year average evens out the ups and downs. Unfortunately, if the income trend has been downward or there was a large gap between amounts, that will reduce the qualifying income derived.

Self-Employment Income

The self-employed borrower with a small or medium sized business is typically the hardest to qualify. The nature of self-employment is to minimize taxable income reporting. So while we often see adequate gross income levels reported, by the time all expenses and tax benefits are deducted, the net income before taxes has been reduced to a level that does not support the two-year average needed to qualify for the loan and home desired. The only solution here is either to buy a smaller home with a larger down payment, or plan ahead and report higher taxable income that year and absorb a higher tax payment. This is the unfortunate Catch-22 of self- employed home buyers stuck between the IRS and mortgage underwriting.

1099s, Tax Returns, Schedule C, Gifts

There are an unlimited number of income and cash scenarios that one encounters when loan qualifying. The general rule is if the income source is a one time or rare event, not reported on tax returns, or from an undocumented or unreported source such as cash side jobs, gifts, etc., then it will NOT be included in your income for loan qualifying. It is still important to your household budget, but just can't be used for the mortgage.

Income vs. Expense Reimbursement

Another area of concern for those with reportable business expenses, whether a direct employee or self-employed, is that most expense reimbursement amounts are either disregarded or discounted by the underwriter. While they show up in your pay, the underwriter correctly assumes most or all of the amount is an actual business related expense, and therefore not available for housing and debt service.

Job History and Consistency

As a home purchase and mortgage are considered a very long-term financial responsibility, underwriters are determining your likelihood of repaying the loan in a consistent manner. The best way is to look to recent job history over the past two to three years. Any gaps in employment, multiple job changes, or income variations will raise red flags and require detailed explanation or may cause your loan request to be declined.

Employment Verification

All sources of income claimed will be verified by documentation such as recent paystubs, W-2 forms, tax returns, or 1099s for self-employment.

Job Transfer

When contemplating a long distance move for job purposes, college graduation, military discharge, etc. and a home purchase is desired, you will need a new employment verification letter of acceptance, including pay level, start date, and job description.

New Employment Verification

This verification letter needs to come from the employing company, on its letterhead, signed by a contact person in HR or your new supervisor, with a phone number that is verifiable by the underwriter. In addition, in most cases you will need to be on the job, having received your first paycheck before being fully approved for the loan. Thus, planning ahead three to six months can be crucial to your move and home purchase timing.

Commuting Long Distances

Some jobs can be far from the home being purchased. This usually happens in order to maintain a previous job, or a buyer wants to be in a favorable home location, but the job is far away. Typically, a job within an hour commute is not an issue, but as the commute gets beyond that, an underwriter may need a full written explanation of the necessity of the long commute and the benefit of doing so. This letter must read well to be acceptable.

Veterans, Retired, Active Duty, Nearing Separation of Duty

Military persons who are either active, recently separated, or retired have unique situations, as their jobs are scheduled to end or they may be re-enlisted. When applying for a mortgage, the underwriter will want an explanation of the intent to separate, re-enlist, or of new job opportunities.

In the case of re-enlistment, for each four years, a letter from the command will likely be required. In the event of separation, the new job must be in place, and a first paycheck received for final qualification. Again, prior planning three to six months out is the way to ensure a successful home purchase.

College or Trade School Graduation

Expected or recent college or trade school graduates will need a job and first paystub in order to be approved. The professional, medical, or trade employee, while very employable in most cases, still needs to be on the job to be loan acceptable. Student loans come into play in the debt consideration phase of underwriting, and have unique issues, which will be discussed later.

Debts

Ahh! Debts are the area that most often trip up home buyers. Credit, credit history, and derogatory items found on credit reports that decrease credit scores below acceptable levels kill more loan requests than all other issues combined, in my experience.

Types of Debt

General categories of debts are consumer debt such as credit cards, loans, lines of credit, auto debt for purchase or lease, student loans, and mortgage debt. These will all show up on the credit report.

Inclusion vs. Exclusion

Credit lines expected to be paid off within 12 months, and generally are not included for qualifying. Those over 12 months will be.

Student Loans, Deferment, Repayment Schedules, Consolidation

Most college students have loans these days. When the student graduates, there is typically a deferment period of 6-12 months. Once the payment begins, it is reported on the borrower's credit report, and becomes a large item to build credit. Often these loans can be consolidated, and the payments reduced.

Charge-Offs

Loan or credit card purchase charge-offs for non-payment or disputed accounts are bad for lenders to see as it indicates a willingness on the applicant's part to fully ignore his or her credit obligations. These can drop a credit score 50-80 points in one month and take one to two years to recover from.

New Debt during Loan Process

Underwriters do not want to see any new or increasing debts just prior to or during the loan process. So any new purchases must be deferred until after the close of the new home purchase.

Credit Cards, Use of, Closing, Excess

Credit cards and auto loans tend to be the backbone of credit in our country. Use of them is quite acceptable and encouraged, as they reflect good financial management. Where they become a problem for underwriters is when there is excessive use. That generally means more than three credit cards, an auto loan, and possible student loan debt, especially when the credit cards are maxed out with a history of high usage. The underwriter assumes the borrower is a high user of debt, which could lead to trouble when a mortgage and homeownership is added to the financial burden.

In addition, excessive debt loads tend to reduce credit scores by 20-40 points even when the payments have been timely. Also, closing of credit lines just prior to or during the mortgage process can reduce credit scores. Again, the best strategy is to manage these events three to six months or more before applying for a mortgage.

Liens, Tax Payments, Debt Counseling, Payment Plans

Additional but less frequent debt/lien problems that need close attention and active management well before the home purchase are lingering items from prior legal issues, child support payments, and debt counseling payment programs. While these can sometimes be worked around by a competent loan officer and cooperative underwriter, they tend to be difficult problems if not addressed until the loan is in process.

Qualifying Ratios

The purpose of financial analysis performed by underwriters is to derive qualifying ratios that meet set guidelines by their respective companies and national housing agencies such as FNMA, VA, and FHA. While there is a range of qualifying debt to income ratios for different loan programs and variables, ultimately there is a narrow range that most loans must adhere to be approved.

Debts

First, the underwriter determines the total debt loan and associated monthly payments, and adds the new assumed loan and housing cost payments to determine total debt level.

Housing

The monthly housing cost of the new purchase is typically the largest monthly recurring debt by far. It is broken into a couple of components.

PITI

Principal, interest, real estate taxes, and home insurance on a monthly prorated basis are the most common components on stand-alone home sales.

HOA / Mello Roos

In most major cities and communities, we now find homeowner associations, special tax pools for schools and local parks, and improvements known as Mello Roos. These fees are pro-rated monthly and added to the housing cost for a total monthly assumed housing cost.

Total Debt

Along with the new housing costs, the underwriter adds the monthly cost of other monthly scheduled debts for a Total Debt Ratio.

Income Calculation: Inclusion

To be included for reportable income we typically see:

W-2 Income

The most common income payment for employees.

Commission

Added back from W-2s or tax returns. This amount is usually averaged from the past two years of reported tax returns.

Schedule C

For self-employed small business owners, the schedule C is a critical part of the income analysis.

Corporations, Ownership, Schedule K

Owners of incorporated businesses, partnerships, or those who may own portions of multiple businesses will require full reporting and analysis of each entity owned, which generates income or losses in some cases.

Rental property

Existing rental property income can be used, but must be reported on tax returns, and generally in place for two years. Tax losses generated by rental property can cause problems by offsetting real income.

Total Debt to Income Ratio

The final result the underwriter is after is the total debt to income ratio, "TDI," or "back end ratio," as it is known.

Deciphering Debt Ratios

The ratios read something like 36/43, which means your housing debt PITI + HOA fees is 36% of your gross monthly income. Your total debts, which include housing plus other reported debts, credit cards, auto loans, student loans, etc., equals 43% of total monthly income. These two ratios in the industry are known as "front" and "back" end ratios, sometimes referred to as "housing" and "total" debt ratios.

Improving Debt vs. Income Changes

There are ways to improve these ratios; for example, by paying off consumer debts, small auto loans, consolidating student loans, etc. Income can be increased in some cases by getting pay raises prior to the loan request, second jobs as long as documented, reporting higher taxable income for the year prior to wanting to buy a home, etc. The thing to keep in mind is that due to the math leverage of the ratios, reducing debt is always more effective than trying to increase income. Obviously, amounts and reasons are important. As with all home and loan planning strategy, working on debts and income levels 6-12 months in advance substantially increases the likelihood of success.

Loan Terms

Interest Rates

Most people are familiar with interest rates on various consumer loans. While credit cards are typically interest only, auto loans tend to have principal and interest components in their payment plans, as do mortgage loans. Most mortgage rates are set by major lenders and bond market activity, which is generally derived from various US Treasury rates.

Fixed vs. Variable

Mortgage loan rates can be fixed, as the most common 30-year fixed rate loan is, and adjustable rate mortgages, or "ARMs," which vary by periods from monthly to annual, reset at the prevailing market rates.

ARMs have reset parameters known as margins, with a floor and ceiling, or maximum rate it can charge at any reset point or over the life of the loan. These features contain the risk of rising interest rates, so as not to put the mortgage borrower at risk of too high a payment at sometime in future years.

Hybrids

There are "hybrid" loans that contain a fixed period of usually three, five, seven, or 10 years, where the rate and payment is fixed for that time frame, and then begins to adjust with regular scheduled resets, typically annually from then on.

Where do Mortgage Rates Begin?

Mortgage rates, as mentioned, are largely set by the mortgage banking industry participants as they derive them from bond and mortgage market activity on a daily basis under complex financial calculations lenders call daily "pricing." Most fixed loan rates are derived initially from US Treasury bonds and bills found in the daily market guides available online or in financial papers like the *Wall Street Journal*.

Points

Loan points, discount points, buy down points, etc. are just a form of interest earned by the lender or mortgage broker. The difference is points are paid at the time of loan closing to the lender, whereas loan interest is earned over time based on remaining balance.

Points can be increased or decreased depending on the borrower's objectives to save money upfront by getting a zero point loan or even a point rebate to cover closing costs, or pay additional points to decrease the loan rate.This decreases the loan payment, and saves money over the life of the loan, at some point recouping the cost of paying the point(s). Generally, the most common option borrowers select is either zero points to save costs, or one point to get the best combination of points and rates without costing too much.

Lender Fees

These fees are charged directly by the funding lender to add to its profit margins and offset origination costs. For disclosure purposes, these are treated the same as points.

Mortgage Interest Rate Buy Downs

Added or extra points to "buy down"are paid to decrease the interest rate and payments.

Loan Types

FHA, VA, Conventional, Conforming, High Balance, Jumbo.

There are a few general categories of home loans that are overseen and regulated by various government, or quasi-government, agencies. The purpose of these loans is to provide home loan credit to differing segments of consumers based on income, credit, down payment, and loan size variables.

High Cost Markets / Agency High Balance Loans

FNMA, the primary national housing agency, has designated an annual market analysis to determine what it calls "conforming" loan size. It can vary annually based on median home prices. The past five to seven years has seen it remain the same at $417,500.

However, in certain major cities and counties it has realized that higher home costs require special loan underwriting treatment, and has given a "high cost" or "agency high balance" loan designation to these costs, which allows more flexible underwriting at higher loan levels on a county-specific level. For example, San Francisco, Hawaii, and New York City tend to have the highest maximum loan amounts nationwide. These are viewable on FNMA's website.

Income Verifying vs. "Stated Income"

There are numerous loan programs that allow for non-traditional methods of proving income known as *no income verifying*, or *stated income* loans. Typically, they have more conservative guidelines as to down payments, cash reserves, self-employment, and other restrictions. They also tend to have much higher interest rates to compensate the lender for the higher risk of not requiring income documentation.

Getting Approved

Now we get to the real strategy to be a successful home buyer.

Getting Prepared

Preparing for loan approval and making offers on homes starts 6-12 months or more before ever applying for loan approval and searching for homes.This is where we get our income (tax returns, paystubs, W-2s collected and reviewed, as well as considering our credit. If unsure of what our credit looks like, we should have our credit report pulled for review.

Most home buyers wait too long to see their credit, and many are surprised by what they see. The buyer should start budgeting if he has not been, and become fully aware of what his monthly costs and income are. Before searching for homes, it is important to start with the question "How much housing cost can I comfortably afford with my income and debts?" If this needs adjusting, 12 months beforehand is the time to start tweaking it by paying off debts, asking for pay raises, getting new jobs, etc.

Prequalifying

Once the home buyer has collected his list of financial and credit related information, it is time to talk to the lender and get prequalified. Basically, this is using an experienced loan officer or automated underwriting system (AUS) like www.eprequal.com to ask relevant questions and provide answers about income, debts, assets, employment, etc. The answers are entered into the AUS, and quickly analyzed according to industry guidelines and loan product selection.

Assuming a positive result, we can move forward with a full loan underwriting and review of the documents needed by the lender. In the event of an initial decline, we can review the reasons to discover whether it was related to income, credit issues, cash needs, time on the job, etc. Most of the time, the motivated homebuyer can find a way to adjust and move forward or he would likely not be this far along in the home buying search.

Underwriters Preapproval

The second level of loan approval is called pre-approval. This is typically the result of the underwriter actually reviewing all documents provided and confirming the AUS results.

Conditional Approval

The preapproval is also known as a conditional approval, as the result delivers long list of conditions that must be met and documents that may still need to be provided and reviewed to get to final approval.

Final Approval

Final approval is more of a process than an event. Once all borrower documents and loan product details have been reviewed and confirmed, and the buyer's purchase contract has been accepted, the property appraised, and the homeowner association has checked the appraisal, the underwriter is ready to let the loan go to the final steps, including drawing up the loan documents to be sent to escrow for buyer signing.

Funding

When loan documents have been signed, notarized, and final figures and all parties' documents received by escrow, the lender will send a wire or fund the loan.

Recording

When this final day arrives, the escrow and title transfer is ready to be completed. The escrow or title company sends the signed grand deed to the county recorder's office for recording as a public notice that the property has transferred ownership. This is the final event that solidifies the new owner's right to occupy and move in.

Determining Maximum Loan Qualifying and Home Purchase Price Range

We are now ready to show a simple example of how qualifying ratios are calculated for a positive loan approval. We will assume a simple 20% down payment purchase loan on a home price of $300,000, for example. Using a conforming FNMA / conventional 30-year fixed rate, the qualifying analysis looks something like this:

Loan Prequalifying Analysis (Worksheet 1**)**

CHAPTER 3
FINDING AND NEGOTIATING YOUR DREAM HOME

This is not a shopping trip to the mall! It is complex, and requires the team of people you will rely on. The only real choice you have is the Realtor you chose and the home you make an offer on. The rest is built around large teams of interrelated parties, each looking out for you, but in business in their own right. So be aware, and be a team player to get best results.

Now that we have successfully received our loan pre-qualification, or even better, our preliminary underwriter preapproval, we have selected our Realtor to be the team manager on our behalf, we are ready to search for homes and make offers.

Search

There are numerous ways to search for homes that meet your needs. One is to drive around until you are cross-eyed. This is fun to do on a sunny day, and a great way to get to know areas and neighborhoods. It's also probably the least effective way to really find the right home.

Online vs. Public

Consumer real estate web sites such as Zillow, Tulia, Realtor.com, and others are easy access, anonymous ways to begin your search. These public online websites get daily data feeds from realtor associations and real estate companies, as well as some input directly from sellers and independent agents. The number of active listings nationally varies, but these websites probably cover 80% of currently or recently active listings.

The problem is that not all realtor associations feed to them, and as of mid-2015, Zillow and Trulia have been cut off from the primary feed source, ListHub, and will need to work hard and fast to replace those feeds by going directly to the thousands of national real estate firms and associations to replace them. In addition, the data can be outdated, and it no longer updates once the property goes into escrow until it closes, which can be one to three months. So a rather larger percentage of listings seen are no longer available for purchase.

Private or RealtorSearch Tools

Realtors nationwide have proprietary home search systems or multiple list systems (MLS) they use to get up-to-the minute complete data, status, viewing instructions, agent comments, etc.

Many agents these days provide website access to homebuyers to these MLS sites through their personal or company websites. Some require registering to view them, some do not. These are direct feeds from their local MLS, and will typically be complete and up-to-date for everything available in a given market area.

MLS Public Feeds

With the proliferation of easy access Internet tools, most local realtor associations these days have public search tools that allow homebuyers to search their local MLS listings. These tend to be current and complete.

Search Parameters

Now that we are pre-approved for a price range and loan amount, the best way to quickly narrow down your home search is by area, then price range, then home styles such as bedrooms, bathrooms, number of stories, yard size, etc. With these specific search parameters, you can narrow your search down to a manageable number of properties to view and write offers on. Typically, if your final list of homes is greater than 20 or so, you are probably not close to being ready to write offers.

Previewing

With a reasonable list of homes to view, it is now time to get inside some and "preview" them, as we say. The goal is to quickly view them, and narrow the field down to five or less homes that really appeal to you, are in your price range, and that you are ready to offer on and negotiate for. So, it's time to find an agent if you have not already done so.

Selecting the Right Realtor

Friends, Family, Part-Timers

One of the first things first-time home buyers do is turn to those they already know to help them. If that person is a part-timer, not familiar with the area, or has limited experience, you are doing yourself a disservice by using him or her, and it will cost you time and money—guaranteed! Save the friendships for less major financial decisions in life, like where to go for dinner. Leave real estate negotiation for professional, full-time agents. You win, and they deserve it.

What Makes a Professional Agent?

There are a few easy-to-know things about a real estate agent that can quickly tell you if he or she is professional and deserves your business. Referrals are good, but you still must answer these questions.

Local Knowledge

Does your agent live and work in the areas you are interested in? Let's say they should work or live— preferably both—within 10 miles of the communities you are looking in.

Experience

Experience can be hard to gauge for a fist-time buyer, but a rule of thumb is that he or she preferably has five years' experience, and has done at least 20 transactions. The absolute minimum should be two years of active selling, with 10 transactions closed.

Communication, Availability

Some of the qualities we look for are just good, common sense business skills. Good communication skills with you and the other parties involved are a must. If you find an agent who is unresponsive, does not fully answer questions, or is just rude or impatient, run! Likewise, he or she should indicate a willingness to be readily available during business days and weekends for viewing homes.

FSBOs

Every first-time home buyer believes in his heart that there is a way to get a "killer" deal out there somewhere, and that by searching far and wide enough, there is the one deal everyone else has overlooked, which is perfect for them. This always leads to For Sale by Owner properties, or FSBO, for short.

Having owned 10 homes myself, and closed 1,500 mortgage and real estate transactions for buyers and owners, I can tell you this is the biggest fallacy in the business for numerous reasons. First, recognize that there are hundreds of buyers and agents in any given area looking for good deals, so the likelihood of a fist-time buyer finding one is slim at best. Next, the reason sellers elect to go FSBO is they typically are trying to bypass agents and selling commissions, and as such, are highly unlikely to turn around and give the savings to the buyer. Their goal is to keep it all themselves, so the buyer hasn't saved much, if anything.

Then we have to worry about two untrained parties attempting to sidestep the normal procedures, processes, and parties to these complex and costly transactions. Buying a FSBO can be a disaster waiting to happen, in my opinion. In addition, there is a fair amount of legal risk, primarily on the shoulders of the buyer, something that no first time buyer should assume. There's a reason the term "buyer beware" exists.

Last, the homebuyer has a whole list of transactional needs that he cannot hope to know about without guidance and assistance from a professional agent. Less than 5% of homes sold are FSBO. If it worked well, everyone would to it. Bottom line, use an agent to represent you, and stay away from FSBOs.

Offers / Terms / Negotiation

Now comes the fun part! Negotiating for price and terms. This area is covered in detail in our advance seminar and coursework, but here is a brief outline of the areas the buyer will be exposed to and have negotiating power in, with the benefit, naturally, of their professional, experienced real estate agent.

Price

First and foremost, price starts with the listing price. Based on other recent sales, and an assumption of some sort of customary discount, the buyer can negotiate this down to between 3-10% off the listing price.

Terms

Terms can mean many things. The purchase offer contract most realtors use will have a series of terms and contingencies that are standard and can be negotiated. These include:

Deposits

Good faith deposits can run from $500 up to $10,000 or more. Since they are typically refundable up to just before closing due to unforeseen circumstances, most listing agents (sellers) do not ask for much. My recommendation is go for $2,500 on the average priced deal.

Escrow Period

The escrow period is the number of days the process will take from the date of the accepted offer, or open escrow date, until the recording or close date. Typically, this is 30 days. For some loan types or special circumstances, the buyer can request longer, say 45 to 60 days. Most sellers will balk at escrow period requests for over 60 days. They do not want to take their home off the market that long in the event you can't close, and they also have moving and other financial needs to address.

Costs / Expenses

(See addendum CC for a detailed breakdown of typical closing costs.) Closing costs are an area that is confusing and requires discussion up-front as to the types, amount, and ways to minimize or have them paid by the seller, the agents, or the lender. In our seminars and online training modules, we discuss in detail how to understand them and get them reduced, or paid for entirely. Don't miss it!

Selection of Closing Services

The selection of closing services, like escrow, title, reports, home warranty companies, etc., can sometimes be requested by the buyer. Normally they are dictated by the seller (actually the seller's agent), and are best left to their needs as a token gesture. There are other reasons why they select them, and we go over these in our advanced training seminars.

Inspections

Home inspections are the buyer's choice, and should be used to determine the specific condition of the home and all appliances.

Appraisals

Every home purchase with financing requires an appraisal, which supports the purchase price by comparing recent sales of similar homes in the immediate area known as comparables, or "comps." The appraiser is selected by the lender through an appraisal management system. The homebuyer will not typically ever meet the appraiser. Most appraisal fees cost $400-$500, or more, depending on the price and complexity.

Contingencies

After the initial offer is accepted, the buyer is afforded contingencies for such things as the home inspection, the appraisal, review of any homeowner association documents, review of a title company report, and finally, their lender's loan final approval. Once those have been completed, and confirmed by the buyer, then they are essentially in a hard escrow, and fully expected to close by all parties unless something big comes up. At this point, the buyer's deposit could be at risk under some circumstances.

Extensions

Buyers can sometimes negotiate for contingency or contract extensions, if the seller is willing. This can be for loan needs, or other last minute bumps. Usually these extensions are going to be for only a few days to a week, at which point the seller has the option to decline the request and cancel the contract if he thinks it is in his interest to do so. Most sellers prefer to allow the extension request and hope to close soon rather than starting over again in a new market time and with an unknown buyer.

Costs, Fees, Allocations

Closing costs, various party fees, and the allocation of costs to seller and buyer are a huge area of discussion and some negotiation. (See addendum 12 for a detailed breakdown of typical closing costs.)

HUD 1 Closing Cost Schedule

The escrow company draws up a schedule of closing costs for each side, based on input from buyer and seller support services, lender charges, taxing authority charges, etc. These are updated throughout, and will become quite accurate in the last week of the transaction, allowing the buyer to know closely what his cash-to-close requirement will be.

Cash to Close

Escrow will provide the buyer's cash target to complete the transaction, and will refer to this as cash to close. This is the difference between the purchase price, less the loan amount plus the deposit and the total closing costs. This net figure will be the amount the buyer will wire or bring to escrow a day or two before the final close date.

Closing Cost Credits

There are numerous sources of credits to the buyer for any home purchase. The source of these credits can come from relatives, special first-time homebuyer incentive programs offered by the state, lender, or sometimes employer programs. But most often they come from the parties to the transaction who may have a financial incentive or tactic to pay for some or all of the buyer's closing costs.

These include:

Sellers

Sellers will often agree to pay closing costs from their sale proceeds. What they are really doing is setting their sale price to cover these. What sellers care about is not the selling price itself, but the net proceeds they walk away with. Thus, a price increase can allow for additional funds to pay buyers' costs. The industry has allowed this practice, within bounds.

Agent(s)

The buyer's real estate agent is allowed by law in most states, and in some cases will give a commission credit to the buyer through escrow to pay for certain closing costs or move-in costs. This can range from a few hundred dollars to thousands of dollars, which some agents offer to get buyers to work with them. Since real estate commissions on even average transactions can run over $10,000 or more, the agent is able to share some and still have a profitable and satisfied client.

Lender rebates

Most mortgage lenders have loan and pricing options that allow for rebates to the borrower to cover closing costs. These can be thousands of dollars, depending on the loan size and need.

Home Warranty

Home warranties are insurance policies that cover appliances, pools, air conditioners, etc. They are typically offered as first-year coverage by the seller, as a way to give the buyer peace of mind that he is not buying broken or substandard home appliances. These policies will pay out for repairs or new equipment in the first 12 months if needed, for a small cost—usually around $50 per incident. The cost to the seller is typically $400-$500 depending on coverage. The new homeowner can elect to renew after the first year, if he desires, at his own cost.

Hazard Insurance

All homeowners will carry some sort of disaster insurance for their homes. Even cash buyers and those with no mortgage want to protect their investment against fire, water damage, tree damage, accidents, etc. The buyer requiring a mortgage will be required to carry insurance at a rate the lender approves, to ensure replacement cost of the home in the event of a major fire or other damage. However, most standard homeowner's policies do not cover earthquake or flood damage from rivers and lakes. That is extra coverage, and usually optional at the buyer's desire.

CHAPTER 4
ESCROW / TITLE

Two closing service providers that most people know nothing of until they are in a purchase transaction are the escrow (or closing) company, and the title insurance company. In some states these two functions are managed within the same company, and in some states and they are separate companies working together to benefit both seller and buyer equally.

What is Escrow?

The role of the escrow company, (not to be confused with a borrower's escrow account for taxes and insurance on the new loan), is directed by the escrow officer, and is that of a neutral third party firm that receives and manages the financial and ownership documents being transferred from seller, buyer, and all third party service providers in the transaction. So for example, the seller and buyer contract is sent to escrow to be confirmed as to the terms agreed upon, timing, each party's responsibility, etc. The buyer's good faith deposit is sent to their account as escrow for safekeeping until closing. Lender documents are sent to escrow for final buyer signing, and notarizing, third party documents like homeowner's association documents are sent to escrow for distribution to each side.

All closing costs, fees, and billings for appraisals, inspections, warranties, etc., are sent to escrow for management and accounting for final payment and distribution at closing. The final escrow steps serve to receive the funds from the buyer's lender and to ensure that each respective party gets the amounts due him or her. The final step is to send the sellers grant deed and new loan trust deed to the county recorder to make an official public statement that the property has been sold, and state who the new owner is. Then the account is closed out with a Final Settlement Statement and a federally required form known as a HUD 1.

What is Title Insurance?

Title owner insurance, like it sounds, is an insurance policy for the owner to ensure he has clear title, meaning no liens or encumbrances that could jeopardize his claim to the property. A second version of the insurance policy is to benefit the lender to ensure there are no liens in front of its first deed of trust that would jeopardize its claim in the event of the need to foreclose on the property for nonpayment of the loan.

The title company's role is to oversee title-related documents, notarized signatures on transfer documents, or any liens against the property. The title company also ensures that the correct owners and lien holders know who each other are by closely watching every document that is recorded against a property at the county recorder. The title company will generally pay out for any claims against the property that were missed by them if it has been recorded in public. Private or unrecorded liens cannot be insured against because there is no way of know of their existence. The title company works very closely with the escrow company, and in many cases the two roles are under one company to allow for efficiencies and oversight.

Choices

Escrow and title services can be provided by a range of companies and service formats. Normally the listing agent selects these to control the seller's risks of non-closure on the buyer's part and the need to closely monitor the buyer's progress to closing. The buyer can always ask to select these, but most buyers, especially first time buyers, have little knowledge of them, and the agents typically respect the seller's need to select these critical services.

Process

The escrow process is a complex series of multi-party steps and documents that must follow a fairly rigid format. The details of that are better left to a more in-depth discussion with a loan officer, realtor, or in our premium courses.

Milestones

Like any complex project, the escrow company has a process, and milestones it must adhere to so that the transaction closes on or before the date agreed to in the purchase contract. Failure to hit these milestones by escrow or any of the parties involved can jeopardize the close date, and potentially the whole transaction. Missed closing dates cause high levels of stress on all parties, and typically cost money for both seller and buyer for numerous applicable pro-rated expenses, which are incurred daily.

CHAPTER 5
CLOSING AND OCCUPANCY

Now that the day of closing has come, it is time to finish and move in.

Recording

The final act of acknowledgement of transfer is the recording of the grant deed transferring ownership from seller to buyer, and the recording of the lender's Trust Deed, which is evidence that the property is held as collateral against repayment of the mortgage.
The recording of the documents takes place at the county recorder's office, and is then made public for review by anyone with a need to know about the transaction and new owner information. The recorded documents are available to the owner for viewing or printing at any time.

Utility Service Transfers

On the day of closing, either the seller's agent, or most likely the buyer or his agent should contact all local utilities, cable, and trash services and transfer billing to the new owner's name. Typically, the seller or seller's agent will provide a list of the names and agencies to contact.

CHAPTER 6
REPAIRS / REMODELING / MAINTENANCE

Now that you own it, assuming no fraud or cover-ups on the part of the sellers, you are responsible for any repairs, remodeling, or maintenance that comes up from day one forward. It is not like buying a car or consumer item—there is no going back to the store, dealer, or any right of return. In egregious cases, the buyer could sue, but it is messy for all parties, and should be reserved for large problems, and as a last, worst case resort.

Before offering on the property, a buyer should have developed a summary plan and budget of some sort for repairs and remodeling work to be performed. That way, you know how much, and when, large amounts of additional funds may be needed to get it into the condition desired. A regular maintenance schedule should be worked up for everything from landscaping to appliance reviews, to periodic full home inspections, by a qualified inspector to ensure the home keeps its value for future financing or sale needs.

CHAPTER 7
WORKSHEETS AND ADDENDUMS

(See end of book addendums and download link.)

Budgeting -Addendum 1

Application –Addendum 2

Credit Report Sample –Addendum 3

Prequalification Analysis – Addendum 4

DU Sample – Addendum 5

Underwriter Summary Sample – Addendum 6

Underwriter List of Items Required – Addendum 7

Purchase Contract – Addendum 8

Offer / Counter-offer – Addendum 9

Walk-through – Addendum 10

Warranty Sample – Addendum 11

Closing Statement – Addendum 12

CHAPTER 8
DISCOUNTS, REBATES, CLOSING COST CREDITS

Tips and Strategies to receive $20,000 or more in credits, rebates, and down payment assistance programs.

Join our Premium Subscriber program for thousands of dollars' worth of free offers, tips, and strategies. Get all these plus access to our top home buying strategists who will teach you in-depth ways on how to make offers and negotiate the best possible deal, how to get loan-approved, and how to find the right home for you.

Credit Report - Get a free credit report with every loan pre-approved through **ePrequal.com**

Loan Pre-qualification – Get a free prequalification at www.ePrequal.com

Appraisal - Free appraisal when you subscribe to our premium service.

Closing Cost Credits – Learn how to get $2,000 to $5,000 and more in closing cost credits.

Down Payment Assistance

Learn about no repayment down payment assistance

programs that can provide 2%-5% down payment for thousands of dollars which you never repay!

Credit Counseling / Repair

Learn how to clean up your credit, remove bad credit items, and increase your credit scores so you can easily qualify for A-grade credit mortgages

CHAPTER 9
NEWSLETTER AND FOLLOW-UP TOPICS

Coaching

For live personalized coaching, subscribe to our Premium services.

Apply Now

To get loan-approved and be ready to make offers, complete this application and return it to us by email at GetPreapproved@ePrequal.com, or go directly to www.ePrequal.com, answer the simple prequalifying questions, and we will take it from there.

Agency Agreement

If you would like us to assist you with your home search and purchase process, please complete our simple Agency Agreement so we can legally represent you.

Newsletter

Subscribe to our free monthly newsletter for updates and discussions on:

- Mortgage rates / terms

- Monthly home sales trends in your market area
- Offer / negotiation tips
- Deal killers - what to avoid

CHAPTER 10
PREMIUM LIVE EDUCATION SEMINARS

Our live web case education seminars, take you step-by-step through the process, from getting ready to buy, to getting loan pre-approved, to searching and negotiating for your home, all the way to following it through the escrow process and closing. Our Home Buyer Service Instructors will mentor you from A to Z.

Don't be made a fool of, or allow yourself to be swindled by agents, lenders, or sellers when buying your dream home. We will help you get your money back many times over with our field-tested negotiating tactics and strategies. We guarantee it, or we refund your money! Call today at**888-930-4223**, or visit us at SimpleStepsHome.com

Module I – Loan Approval and Rate Locks

Module II - Search and Negotiate for your Home.

Module III – Manage and Close your Transaction.

Module IV – Repairs, Remodeling, Maintenance.

ABOUT THE AUTHOR

David Van Waldick has 25 years of experience in banking, finance,real estate, and business management. With strong experience across sales and marketing, financial analysis, strategic business planning, and advisory services.

- President/Owner **Western Realty / Finance**
- CEO / Developer **ePrequal.com** Home Buyer mortgage instant pre-approval system.
- Closed 1,500 mortgage and real estate sales for over $1 billion.
- Educator and Seminar speaker.
- WRFCO, LLC – Media and Technology.
- Expert financial analysis and valuation skills.
- Experienced in management and operations.

Corporations worked for: Central Federal Savings, Crocker Bank, Wells Fargo Bank, Key Bank, First American Title.

Education: B.S. Finance – San Diego State University
Military: US Navy, 1975-80

Email: Dave@WRFCO.com
Phone: 888-930-4223

SIMPLE GUIDE BOOKS BY DAVID VAN WALDICK

1. A Simple Guide -How to Buy a Home

2. A Simple Guide - How to Retire Wealthy

3. A Simple Guide - How to Grow your Small Business

4. A Simple Guide - How to Write a Book and Be Viewed as an Expert in Your Field

CAN I ASK A FAVOR?

If you enjoyed this book, and found it useful or otherwise, then I'd really appreciate it if you would post a short review on Amazon. I do read all the reviews personally so that I can continually write what people want to know about.

If you'd like to leave a review then please visit this link: HOME BUYING: Master the Process:

Thanks for your support!

Addendum 1 - Monthly Budgeting

Household Budget w/ Qualifying Ratios		
Income #1:	$	6,000
Income #2:	$	3,500
Income #3:	$	750
Total Income:	$	10,250
Expenses:		
New Housing Estimate		
Mortgage	2400	
RE Taxes	250	
Insurance	80	
Homeowner Fees	80	
Total Housing:	$	2,810
Credit Cards	50	
Utilities	125	
Phone	25	
Cable	37	
Food	500	
Cell Phone	100	
Clothing	0	
Water	50	
Trash	18	
Entertainment	25	
Medical Insurance	59	
Child Care	450	
Life Insurance / Investing	150	
Miscellaneous	69	
Total Household Expenses:	$	1,658
Total Living Expenses:	$	4,468
Residual Income:	$	5,782

Addendum 2 - Prequalification Analysis Example

I. PURCHASE LOAN TERMS	
Property Type:	**Detached**
Loan Type:	30 Year Fixed
Purchase Price:	$350,000
% Down Payment	20.0%
$ Down Payment	$70,000
First TD Amount:	$280,000
Loan Term (Mos.)	360
Loan Origination Points:	0.000%
1st Year Payment Interest Rate:	3.750%
Principal & Interest:	$1,297
2nd Trust Deed (x%):	0
2nd TD Payment (Int. only):	0
Real Estate Taxes:	292
HOA Fee:	150
Fire / Hazard Insurance:	80
PMI Payments:	0
TOTAL PAYMENT (PITI):	**$1,818**
II. PRE-QUALIFYING ANALYSIS	
DEBT PAYMENTS (Monthly)	
Mortgage Pmt. (PITI):	$1,818
Auto Pmts.:	$350
Credit Cards:	$150
Other Debts:	$0
	$2,318
QUALIFYING MONTHLY INCOME	
Required Income #1:	5,500
Income #2:	0
Income #3:	$0
TOTAL INCOME:	**$5,500**
III. QUALIFYING RATIOS	
Housing Pmt.:	**33.1%**
Total Debts:	**42.2%**
Qualified to Purchase:	Yes & Go!
After Tax Pmt. (.15% Tax Rate):	**$1,500**

For a free packet of additional addendums and worksheets that will assist you in becoming a knowledgeable homebuyer, download:
http://www.simplestepshome.com/

Addendum 3: Loan Application

Addendum 4: Credit Report Sample

Addendum 5: DU Automated Underwriting Sample

Addendum 6: Underwriter Summary Sample

Addendum 7: Underwriter List of Items Required

Addendum 8: Purchase Contract

Addendum 9: Offer / Counter-offer

Addendum 10: Walk-through

Addendum 11: Warranty Sample

Addendum 12: Closing Statement / HUD 1.

www.ingramcontent.com/pod-product-compliance
Lightning Source LLC
Chambersburg PA
CBHW070229210526
45168CB00019B/1205